REAL WORLD MATHS

Win a
GRAND PRIX

**Wendy Clemson, David Clemson
and Jonathan Noble**

© TickTock Entertainment Ltd 2004, 2011

This revised edition published in 2011 by TickTock.

First published in Great Britain as *Using Maths Win a Grand Prix* in 2004 by TickTock.

The Pantiles Chambers, 85 High Street, Tunbridge Wells, Kent, TN1 1XP, UK.

ISBN 978 1 84898 533 9

Printed in China

10 9 8 7 6 5 4 3 2 1

With thanks to our consultants: Jenni Back and Liz Pumfrey from the NRICHProject,
Cambridge University and to Debra Voege and Lorna Cowan.

Additional thanks to Kerry Johnson, who supplied revisions for this latest edition,
ensuring all material is current.

Publisher's note: We have included the imperial measurements miles and mph,
as both are commonly used in some countries. Where necessary, some conversions
from metric to imperial have been rounded down or up, or approximations given.

WENDY CLEMSON

Wendy is experienced in working with and for children, and has been writing full-time since 1989. Her publications, which now exceed one hundred, have been written for children and sometimes their parents and teachers. In her many maths books, the aim is always to present the reader with challenges that are fun to do.

DAVID CLEMSON

David has wide-ranging experience as a writer and educationalist. His publications list is prodigious. In collaboration with Wendy, David has worked on many maths books for children. He is fascinated by maths and logic puzzles and is keen for the reader to enjoy them too.

JONATHAN NOBLE

Jonathan is Grand Prix Editor for *AUTOSPORT Magazine*. Jonathan began his career by winning a young motor racing journalist's prize for interviewing David Coulthard, before David was famous. Jonathan has also worked for *The Daily Telegraph*, *REUTERS* and *The European*.

CONTENTS

NUMERACY WORK COVERED IN THIS BOOK:

CALCULATIONS:
Throughout this book there are opportunities to practise **addition, subtraction, multiplication** and **division** using both mental calculation strategies and pencil and paper methods.

NUMBERS AND THE NUMBER SYSTEM:
- DECIMALS: pg. 19
- WORKING WITH NUMBERS TO 10,000: pg. 6
- ROUNDING: pg. 9

SOLVING 'REAL LIFE' PROBLEMS:
- CHOOSING THE OPERATION: pgs. 6, 10, 23, 24
- MEASURES: pgs. 6, 16, 23, 24
- TIME: pgs. 10, 18, 19, 21

HANDLING DATA:
- PICTOGRAMS: pg. 8
- USING TABLES/CHARTS/DIAGRAMS: pgs. 6, 7, 9, 16, 19, 23, 26

MEASURES:
- CALENDARS: pg. 7
- ESTIMATING: pg. 12
- PERIMETER: pg. 17
- TIME (reading from 12-hour digital clocks): pg. 10
- TIMETABLES: pgs. 10, 20
- USING METRIC/IMPERIAL MEASUREMENTS: pgs. 6, 9, 12, 16, 17, 23, 24
- VOCABULARY (time): pgs. 10, 18, 20, 21

SHAPE AND SPACE:
- ANGLES: pg. 15
- NETS: pg. 27

Supports the maths work taught at Key Stage 2/3

HOW TO USE THIS BOOK

Maths is important in the lives of people everywhere. We use maths when we play a game, ride a bike, go shopping – in fact, all the time! Everyone needs to use maths at work. You may not realise it, but a racing driver would use maths to win a Grand Prix! With this book you will get the chance to try lots of exciting maths activities using real life data and facts about Formula One racing. Practise your maths and numeracy skills and experience the thrill of what it's really like to be a top racing driver.

This exciting maths book is very easy to use – check out what's inside!

Fun to read information about Formula One Grands Prix and the lives of racing drivers.

MATHS ACTIVITIES

Look for the
DRIVER ASSESSMENT.
You will find real life maths activities and questions to try.

To answer some of the questions, you will need to collect data from a DATA BOX. Sometimes, you will need to collect facts and data from the text or from charts and diagrams.

Be prepared! You will need a pen or pencil and a notebook for your workings and answers.

PLANNING YOUR PIT STOPS

During a race the cars need to make **pit stops**. The drivers pull off the track into a special area called the **pits**. During pit stops, the cars are refuelled, the tyres are changed and the teams' pit crews make other checks. **Formula One** racing teams have to decide how many pit stops they will make in a race. They also need to work out how much fuel to carry. If you have lots of fuel on board, the car will weigh more which will slow you down. However, if you only carry a small amount of fuel, you will have to make more pit stops to refuel, which will cost you vital seconds. Try the next DRIVER ASSESSMENT and decide on your team's **strategy**.

DRIVER ASSESSMENT

In the DATA BOX you will see information about how much fuel your car will use per lap. You will also see the choices you have for when you can take a pit stop to refuel. Use the information to answer these questions:

1) If you choose the one PIT STOP option, how much fuel do you need at the start of the race?

2) If you make 2 pit stops, how much fuel will you put in at your first pit stop?

3) If you make 3 pit stops, how much fuel do you need to put in at each of the stops?

(Remember, your car should be completely empty of fuel as it goes into the pits.)

RACE FACT
For every 10 kilograms of fuel that the car carries, it loses 0.3 seconds of time per lap. So as the fuel is used up, the car can race around the track faster.

16

Fun to read racing facts.

DATA BOX

If you see one of these boxes, there will be important data inside that will help you with the maths activities.

MATHS ACTIVITIES

Feeling confident?
Try these extra
CHALLENGE QUESTIONS.

IF YOU NEED HELP...

TIPS FOR MATHS SUCCESS

On pages 28–29 you will find lots of tips to help you with your maths work.

ANSWERS

Turn to pages 30–31 to check your answers.
(Try all the activities and questions before you take a look at the answers.)

GLOSSARY

On page 32 there is a glossary of motor racing words and a glossary of maths words. The glossary words appear **in bold** in the text.

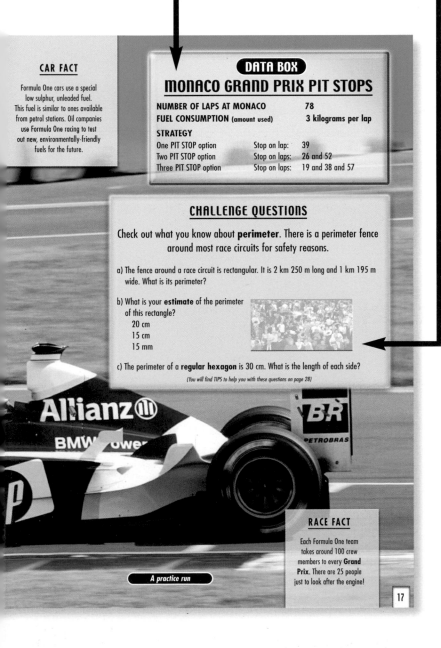

CAR FACT

Formula One cars use a special low sulphur, unleaded fuel. This fuel is similar to ones available from petrol stations. Oil companies use Formula One racing to test out new, environmentally-friendly fuels for the future.

DATA BOX
MONACO GRAND PRIX PIT STOPS

NUMBER OF LAPS AT MONACO	78
FUEL CONSUMPTION (amount used)	3 kilograms per lap

STRATEGY

One PIT STOP option	Stop on lap:	39
Two PIT STOP option	Stop on laps:	26 and 52
Three PIT STOP option	Stop on laps:	19 and 38 and 57

CHALLENGE QUESTIONS

Check out what you know about **perimeter**. There is a perimeter fence around most race circuits for safety reasons.

a) The fence around a race circuit is rectangular. It is 2 km 250 m long and 1 km 195 m wide. What is its perimeter?

b) What is your **estimate** of the perimeter of this rectangle?
    20 cm
    15 cm
    15 mm

c) The perimeter of a **regular hexagon** is 30 cm. What is the length of each side?

(You will find TIPS to help you with these questions on page 28)

Allianz
BMW ower
BR
PETROBRAS

RACE FACT

Each Formula One team takes around 100 crew members to every **Grand Prix**. There are 25 people just to look after the engine!

A practice run

17

5

THE START OF THE SEASON

Top racing drivers get the chance to travel all over the world. They fly first class, or sometimes in their own jets, they stay in the best hotels or in luxury apartments and they get to meet lots of other celebrities! However, being a racing driver is not all play. On **Grand Prix** weekends, racing drivers have to work hard. There are **strategy** meetings, **press conferences** and **sponsor** functions. In fact the only time the drivers can really relax is when they are in their cars! A new Grand Prix season is about to begin. It is time to take your first DRIVER ASSESSMENT.

DRIVER ASSESSMENT

You are a top racing driver and you live in Monaco. Using the information in the DATA BOX, work out some distances that you will need to travel during the new **Formula One** Grand Prix season.

1) Apart from the race in Monaco, which is the shortest distance and which is the longest distance you will travel to get to a race?
2) What is the difference in distance between travelling to Canada and travelling to Great Britain?
3) How much further is it to Malaysia than to Bahrain.
4) By how many kilometres is the journey to Brazil shorter than the journey to Japan?
5) If you go home to Monaco after each race, how far do you travel in August?

(You will find a TIP to help you with question 2 on page 28)

RACING TEAM FACT

Each Formula One racing team takes 30 000 kg of equipment to every race. This includes three fully-built **chassis**, 17 000 spare parts, ten engines, five gearboxes, 172 wheels, five steering wheels and six helmets!

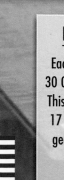

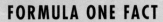

FORMULA ONE FACT

Formula One is a set of rules for single seater racing cars. The cars have to be built to a special set of design specifications, which include safety measures to protect the drivers. A car built to these specifications is a Formula One car, and a race run between these cars is a Formula One Grand Prix.

DATA BOX **THE FORMULA ONE SEASON**

DATE OF RACE	GRAND PRIX OF...	KM from Monaco	
7 March	Australia (Melbourne)	16 404	(10 193 miles)
21 March	Malaysia (Sepang)	10 136 km	(6298 miles)
4 April	Bahrain (Manama)	4313 km	(2680 miles)
25 April	San Marino (Imola)	488 km	(303 miles)
9 May	Spain (Barcelona)	682 km	(424 miles)
23 May	Monaco (Monte Carlo)	0 km	(0 miles)
30 May	Europe (Nürburgring)	901 km	(560 miles)
13 June	Canada (Montreal)	6169 km	(3833 miles)
20 June	USA (Indianapolis)	7376 km	(4583 miles)
4 July	France (Magny-Cours)	731 km	(454 miles)
11 July	Great Britain (Silverstone)	1328 km	(825 miles)
25 July	Germany (Hockenheim)	874 km	(543 miles)
15 August	Hungary (Budapest)	985 km	(612 miles)
29 August	Belgium (Spa-Francorchamps)	1070 km	(665 miles)
12 September	Italy (Monza)	320 km	(199 miles)
26 September	China (Shanghai)	9325 km	(5794 miles)
10 October	Japan (Suzuka)	9862 km	(6128 miles)
24 October	Brazil (Sao Paolo)	9289 km	(5772 miles)

CHALLENGE QUESTIONS

Here is a month in a driver's calendar.

Sunday	Monday	Tuesday	Wednesday	Thursday	Friday	Saturday
				1	PRACTICE 2	Qualifying 3
RACE DAY 4	5	6	7	8	PRACTICE 9	Qualifying 10
RACE DAY 11	12	13	14	15	16	17
18	19	20	21	22	PRACTICE 23	Qualifying 24
RACE DAY 25	26	27	28	29	30	31

Use the information in the DATA BOX to answer these questions:
a) Which month is shown on the calendar?
b) Where is the driver racing on the second Sunday?

GRAND PRIX CIRCUITS

Grand Prix circuits (race tracks) have straights, curves, bends and hairpin bends. All the circuits are very different. Once around a circuit is called a lap. The length of a lap is different from circuit to circuit. Apart from at Monaco, Grands Prix are always run to the least number of laps over 305 kilometres (190 miles). This means the Belgium Grand Prix is only 44 laps, because the laps at that circuit are really long. Other Grands Prix are over 70 laps, because the laps at those circuits are quite short. Get to know the Grand Prix circuits by taking your second DRIVER ASSESSMENT.

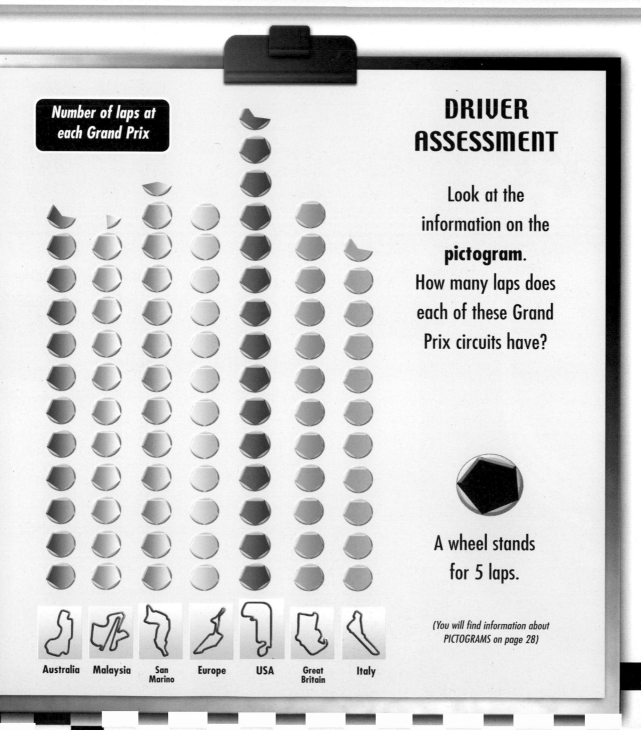

Number of laps at each Grand Prix

Australia Malaysia San Marino Europe USA Great Britain Italy

DRIVER ASSESSMENT

Look at the information on the **pictogram**. How many laps does each of these Grand Prix circuits have?

A wheel stands for 5 laps.

(You will find information about PICTOGRAMS on page 28)

CIRCUIT FACT

The Spa-Francorchamps circuit in Belgium is the longest. The exact length of a lap is 6.973 kms (4.332 miles). The Belgium Grand Prix lasts for 44 laps, which is a total distance of 306.812 kms (190.644 miles).

CIRCUIT FACT

The Monaco circuit is the shortest. A lap measures exactly 3.34 kms (2.08 miles). The total length of the race is 260.52 kms (161.88 miles). The drivers have to race around the track an exhausting 78 times!

DATA BOX
GRAND PRIX CIRCUITS

GRAND PRIX	LAP LENGTH	NUMBER OF LAPS PER GRAND PRIX
AUSTRALIA*	5.3 km (3.3 miles)	?
MALAYSIA*	5.5 km (3.4 miles)	?
BAHRAIN	5.4 km (3.4 miles)	57
SAN MARINO*	4.9 km (3 miles)	?
SPAIN	4.6 km (2.9 miles)	66
MONACO	3.3 km (2.1 miles)	78
EUROPE*	5.1 km (3.2 miles)	?
CANADA	4.4 km (2.7 miles)	70
USA*	4.2 km (2.6 miles)	?
FRANCE	4.4 km (2.7 miles)	70
GREAT BRITAIN*	5.1 km (3.2 miles)	?
GERMANY	4.6 km (2.9 miles)	67
HUNGARY	4.4 km (2.7 miles)	70
BELGIUM	7.0 km (4.3 miles)	44
ITALY*	5.8 km (3.6 miles)	?
CHINA	5.5 km (3.4 miles)	56
JAPAN	5.8 km (3.6 miles)	53
BRAZIL	4.3 km (2.7 miles)	71

* The number of laps is missing from some of the circuits. You can work out how many laps these circuits have by using the pictogram on the driver's clipboard.

Malaysian Grand Prix at Sepang.

CHALLENGE QUESTIONS

Look at the lap lengths for each Grand Prix circuit in the DATA BOX.

a) Which circuits have a lap length that is less than Australia, but more than San Marino?

b) If the lap lengths were rounded to the nearest kilometre, which tracks would be 6 kilometres (4 miles) long?

(You will find TIPS to help you with question b on page 28)

RACING TEAMS AND DRIVERS

In order to drive in a **Grand Prix**, a racing driver must have a *Super Licence*. These special licences are only awarded to drivers who have been successful in junior categories, or to drivers who have completed enough kilometres testing a **Formula One** car. Formula One racing is all about teamwork. The **constructors** (the team) design and build the best racing car possible. Then the team's two drivers need to use their skills to win the races on the track. Every season, there are two titles up for grabs – *The Drivers' World Championship* and *The Constructors' Championship*.

DRIVER ASSESSMENT

Racing drivers have to be very fit because driving a Formula One car takes a lot of strength and stamina.

Top drivers can train for up to 5 hours every day.
Look at the stopwatches showing your training times for last season and for this season.

1) In which of your sports have your times improved?
By how many seconds?
2) In which sport has your time got slower? By how many seconds do you need to improve your time to match last season's time?

(You will find a TIP to help you with these questions on page 28)

	Last season	This season
CYCLING 10 km (6 miles)	14:10 minutes seconds	13:55 minutes seconds
RUNNING 1 km (0.6 miles)	03:59 minutes seconds	03:38 minutes seconds
SWIMMING 5 lengths	02:56 minutes seconds	03:02 minutes seconds

CHALLENGE QUESTIONS

Look at your training diary for the season.

a) How many hours a week did you spend in the gym?
b) In total, how many hours did you spend training each week?

(You will find a TIP to help you with these questions on page 28)

MONDAY	9 – 11 gym	4 – 5 swimming
TUESDAY	8 – 9 running	2 – 5:30 gym
WEDNESDAY	8 – 9 running 9 – 10:45 gym	3 – 6:15 swimming
THURSDAY	8 – 10 cycling	3:30 – 5:30 swimming
FRIDAY	9 – 11:20 gym	3 – 5:10 swimming

WILLIAMSF1

CONSTRUCTORS' WORLD TITLES: 9

JUAN PABLO MONTOYA
DATE OF BIRTH: September 20, 1975
DEBUT: Australia 2001
FIRST WIN: Italy 2001

RALF SCHUMACHER
DATE OF BIRTH: June 30, 1975
DEBUT: Australia 1997
FIRST WIN: San Marino 2001

Ralf Schumacher inside his car

RENAULT

CONSTRUCTORS' WORLD TITLES: 0

JARNO TRULLI
DATE OF BIRTH: July 13, 1974
DEBUT: Australia 1997

FERNANDO ALONSO
DATE OF BIRTH: July 29, 1981
DEBUT: Australia 2001
FIRST WIN: Hungary 2003

MCLAREN

CONSTRUCTORS' WORLD TITLES: 8

DAVID COULTHARD
DATE OF BIRTH: March 27, 1971
DEBUT: Spain 1994
FIRST WIN: Portugal 1995

KIMI RAIKKONEN
DATE OF BIRTH: October 17, 1979
DEBUT: Australia 2001
FIRST WIN: Malaysia 2003

Montoya, Coulthard and Raikkonen

BAR

CONSTRUCTORS' WORLD TITLES: 0

JENSON BUTTON
DATE OF BIRTH: January 19, 1980
DEBUT: Australia 2000

TAKUMA SATO
DATE OF BIRTH: January 28, 1977
DEBUT: Australia 2002

FERRARI

CONSTRUCTORS' WORLD TITLES: 13

MICHAEL SCHUMACHER
DATE OF BIRTH: January 3, 1969
DEBUT: Belgium 1991
FIRST WIN: Belgium 1992
DRIVERS' TITLES: 6

RUBENS BARRICHELLO
DATE OF BIRTH: May 23, 1972
DEBUT: South Africa 1993
FIRST WIN: Germany 2000

Michael Schumacher with the cheering Ferrari team

DRIVER FACT

During a race, drivers need to be protected in case they have an accident. They wear special overalls made from a material called Nomex, which can resist fire for 12 seconds. Drivers also wear Nomex underwear, a fireproof balaclava, an ultra strong helmet, fireproof racing gloves and racing boots, which have rubber soles for maximum grip on the pedals.

All the driver and team facts are current as of the end of the 2003 season.

IS YOUR CAR READY TO RACE?

Formula One cars must fit a strict set of technical rules before they are allowed to race. If the car doesn't match up, it will be disqualified! The length, height and weight of the car and the size of its tyres must all fit in with the rules. Safety precautions such as roll bars, leak-resistant fuel tanks and protection for the driver's head and neck are all specified in the rules, and must be fitted. A Formula One car is made up of 80 000 parts, it has more than a kilometre of cable inside and it can cost more than one million pounds!

DRIVER ASSESSMENT

Do you have a feel for what a
Formula One car is like?
*Look at the main picture and the measures
below, then make your **estimate**.*

1) The width of the car is about:

180 mm   **1800 mm**   **18 mm**

2) The length of the car is approximately:

370 cm   **37 000 cm**   **37 cm**

3) The car and its driver weigh at least:

60.5 kg   **6050 kg**   **605 kg**

(You will find information about UNITS OF MEASUREMENT on page 29)

TECHNICAL FACTS

Formula One rules state that the car and its driver have to weigh over
a certain amount. If the car is too light, ballast (heavy stuff), such as
metal, is added to make up the weight. The fit in the car's cockpit is
so tight, that the driver can only get in and out of the car if the
steering wheel is removed!

CHALLENGE QUESTIONS

A Formula One car would take a person about 240 000 hours to build.
(That's about 27 years — if they worked non-stop, day and night!)

a) If 10 people were building the car, how many hours work would that be for each of them ?

b) If 100 people were building the car, how many hours work would that be for each of them?

In real life, it takes a team of 300 people to build a Formula One car.

c) How many hours work is that for each person in the real life team?

d) If each person works for 10 hours a day, how many days would it take to build the car?

(You will find a TIP to help you with these questions on page 28)

Michael Schumacher in his Ferrari.

FORMULA ONE FACT

Formula One cars are closely checked and watched by scrutineers throughout the race weekend. These special officials make sure that the racing teams do not break any rules while they are working on their cars and preparing them for the race.

I t is the weekend of the Monaco **Grand Prix**. At Monaco some of the streets in the city are closed down to make the circuit. The drivers actually race on the normal roads! The cars hurtle past the harbour, past casinos and hotels, up hills, around bends and even through a tunnel. Monaco is one of the most exciting races of the season and one of the most mathematical. The race is won on **strategy** because overtaking is very difficult. Before the start of the race on Sunday, you will need to make lots of important strategy decisions with your team.

DRIVER ASSESSMENT

Before a race the team need to set up the car to make sure it will go as fast as possible. Two of the most important decisions to be made are which gear settings to use and the angle to set the **downforce**, using the car's wings. The gears in a racing car can be adjusted to suit different race conditions.

Downforce

The driver will speed around the Monaco track three times. The wings will be set in a different position each time: LOW, MEDIUM and then HIGH. Look at the diagram of the Monaco circuit and you will see that the track is split into three sectors. The team record how fast the driver does in each sector with each of the downforce settings. Add up the three sector times first for the LOW setting, then for the MEDIUM setting and then the HIGH.

	Sector 1 time in seconds		Sector 2 time in seconds		Sector 3 time in seconds	
LOW setting	19.5	+	37.4	+	18.4	=
MEDIUM setting	19.3	+	37.2	+	18.2	=
HIGH setting	19.6	+	37.1	+	17.9	=

1) Which downforce setting gives the fastest lap time?

Gear settings

The driver will speed around the track another three times. The gears will be set in a different position each time: LOW, MEDIUM and then HIGH. Add up the sector times for the LOW, MEDIUM and HIGH gear settings.

	Sector 1 time in seconds		Sector 2 time in seconds		Sector 3 time in seconds	
LOW setting	19.4	+	37.1	+	17.9	=
MEDIUM setting	19.4	+	37.0	+	18.1	=
HIGH setting	19.5	+	37.1	+	18.2	=

2) Which gear settings give the fastest lap time?

In the tunnel at Monaco.

Monaco Circuit

Sector 1

Sector 3

Tunnel

Sector 2

The car's wings are here!

CHALLENGE QUESTION

The wings on a Formula One car can be adjusted. Low set wings give the least amount of downforce. This allows the car to go faster. When the wings are set high, this gives the car more grip on corners, but more drag, so it is slower on straights. To understand how to set the car's wings, you need to understand **angles**.

Test your knowledge of angles. Which of the angles below is 90°, 60°, 30°, 180°, 45°?

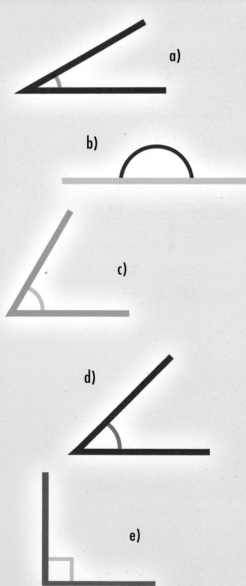

a)

b)

c)

d)

e)

(You will find information to help you with ANGLES on page 28)

During a race the cars need to make **pit stops.** The drivers pull off the track into a special area called the **pits.** During pit stops, the cars are refuelled, the tyres are changed and the teams' pit crews make other checks. **Formula One** racing teams have to decide how many pit stops they will make in a race. They also need to work out how much fuel to carry. If you have lots of fuel on board, the car will weigh more which will slow you down. However, if you only carry a small amount of fuel, you will have to make more pit stops to refuel, which will cost you vital seconds. Try the next DRIVER ASSESSMENT and decide on your team's **strategy.**

DRIVER ASSESSMENT

In the DATA BOX you will see information about how much fuel your car will use per lap. You will also see the choices you have for when you can take a pit stop to refuel. Use the information to answer these questions:

1) If you choose the one PIT STOP option, how much fuel do you need at the start of the race?

2) If you make 2 pit stops, how much fuel will you put in at your first pit stop?

3) If you make 3 pit stops, how much fuel do you need to put in at each of the stops?

(Remember, your car should be completely empty of fuel as it goes into the pits.)

RACE FACT

For every 10 kilograms of fuel that the car carries, it loses 0.3 seconds of time per lap. So as the fuel is used up, the car can race around the track faster.

Formula One cars use a special low sulphur, unleaded fuel. This fuel is similar to ones available from petrol stations. Oil companies use Formula One racing to test out new, environmentally-friendly fuels for the future.

DATA BOX
MONACO GRAND PRIX PIT STOPS

NUMBER OF LAPS AT MONACO   **78**

FUEL CONSUMPTION (amount used)   **3 kilograms per lap**

STRATEGY

One PIT STOP option	Stop on lap:	39
Two PIT STOP option	Stop on laps:	26 and 52
Three PIT STOP option	Stop on laps:	19 and 38 and 57

CHALLENGE QUESTIONS

Check out what you know about **perimeter**. There is a perimeter fence around most race circuits for safety reasons.

a) The fence around a race circuit is rectangular. It is 2 km 250 m long and 1 km 195 m wide. What is its perimeter?

b) What is your **estimate** of the perimeter of this rectangle?
20 cm
15 cm
15 mm

c) The perimeter of a **regular hexagon** is 30 cm. What is the length of each side?

(You will find TIPS to help you with these questions on page 28)

A practice run

RACE FACT

Each Formula One team takes around 100 crew members to every **Grand Prix**. There are 25 people just to look after the engine!

WILL YOU MAKE POLE POSITION?

At the start of a **Grand Prix**, the cars line up in rows. This is called the **grid.** If you are at the front of the grid at the start of the race, you are in *pole position* (the best position). To work out their positions on the grid, the drivers take part in a **qualifying session** the day before the race. One at a time, the cars drive out of the **pits** and make three laps of the circuit. The *flying lap* (the middle lap) is the most important one because the cars are timed. The driver who does the fastest flying lap time will be in pole position!

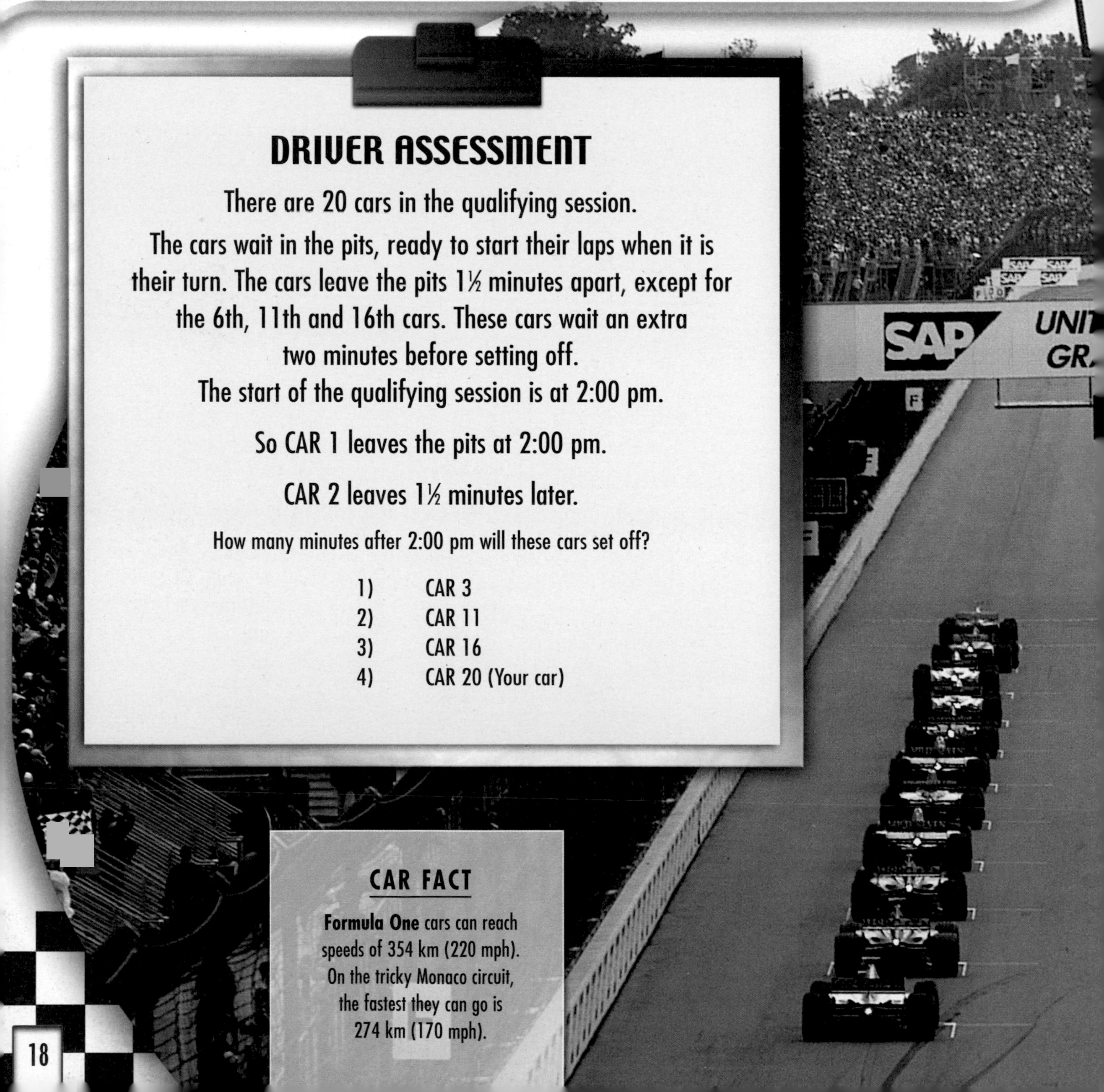

DRIVER ASSESSMENT

There are 20 cars in the qualifying session.

The cars wait in the pits, ready to start their laps when it is their turn. The cars leave the pits 1½ minutes apart, except for the 6th, 11th and 16th cars. These cars wait an extra two minutes before setting off.

The start of the qualifying session is at 2:00 pm.

So CAR 1 leaves the pits at 2:00 pm.

CAR 2 leaves 1½ minutes later.

How many minutes after 2:00 pm will these cars set off?

1) CAR 3
2) CAR 11
3) CAR 16
4) CAR 20 (Your car)

CAR FACT

Formula One cars can reach speeds of 354 km (220 mph). On the tricky Monaco circuit, the fastest they can go is 274 km (170 mph).

The grid at Indianapolis, USA.

CHALLENGE QUESTION

The qualifying session is over and the flying lap times have been used to work out the positions on the grid. Below, you will see the top six cars in formation on the grid. Here are the lap times for the fastest six drivers, including you:

BMW WilliamsF1 driver	74.6 seconds
Ferrari driver	75.1 seconds
YOU	74.8 seconds
McLaren driver	75.0 seconds
Renault driver	74.9 seconds
BAR driver	75.4 seconds

Can you work out which driver is in which car on the grid?

6th

5th

4th

3rd

2nd

POLE POSITION

(You will find some information about PUTTING NUMBERS IN ORDER on page 29)

RACE DAY

It is the morning of the big race. **Formula One** cars have to start the race as they ended their **qualifying session.** The cars must have the same tyres, and the teams are not allowed to add any extra fuel. During a race weekend, the cars are kept in a special compound overnight. On the morning of the race, the teams get their cars back at 8:00 am. There are lots of final checks to be made before your car is due on the **grid** at 1:30 pm. While your team are working on the car, you must prepare for the race. However, you will not have much time to relax – there are TV interviews, the team briefing and the drivers' parade to take part in.

DRIVER ASSESSMENT

The morning of a race is very busy.

Here are some activities a driver has to do:

- Meeting with engineers
- Make final checks on car
- Drivers' parade
- Put on helmet
- Eat breakfast
- Meet reporters

Here are the time slots for these activities:

- 1:50 pm
- 11:30 am
- 12:00 pm
- 8:30 am
- 9:30 am
- 1:20 pm

Can you match the time slots and activities to the photographs?

C

A

D

B

CHALLENGE QUESTION

It is 10:20 am. Your team still have a number of repairs to make before the race. They have three hours and ten minutes left to complete the work.

This is how long each repair will take:

Seat-belt — 12 minutes
Accelerator pedal — 58 minutes
Rear suspension — 1 hour 9 minutes
Front bargeboard — 47 minutes

Will your car be ready in time?

THE START OF THE RACE

- 30 minutes to the start: cars leave the **pits**, make a lap of the track and then line up in their grid positions.

- 15 minutes to the start: the pit exit is closed.

- 10 minutes to the start: everyone must leave the grid except the drivers, team technical staff and officials.

- 5 minutes to the start: a series of lights at the grid now signals the countdown to the start of the race.

- 3 minutes to the start

- 1 minute to the start: cars start engines.

- 15 seconds to the start

- The cars make a *formation lap* to warm up their tyres. The cars stay in their grid positions.

- When all the cars are back on the grid, the final countdown begins.

- 5 seconds

- 4 seconds

- 3 seconds

- 2 seconds

- 1 second

- The race director will now choose when to start the race. When all the red lights go out, the race has started.

(You will find some information about PATTERNS IN MATHS on page 29)

CAN YOU KEEP YOUR COOL IN THE RACE?

You're off – now anything can happen, from a mechanical failure on your car to a dangerous crash. Whatever happens, it will happen fast and at high speed! During a race, **Formula One** drivers need to concentrate hard and be ready to deal with lots of different problems. The drivers also need to keep a look out for different flags. The flags show the drivers what is happening in the race. Try a lap of the Monaco circuit and see if you can deal with hazards on the track and problems with your car.

DRIVER ASSESSMENT

Look at the Monaco track on these pages.

If every place on the track is 1 second of time, a full lap will be 60 seconds.

You are going to use a dice to give you an idea of what it feels like to be in a race and suddenly be presented with an unexpected hazard.

• Write down your ideal lap time of 60 seconds. Now throw the dice and start moving around the track.

• If you land on a place with a flag, check what it means and do what it says. This will add seconds to your lap time, or make it faster by subtracting seconds.

How fast was your lap time?

Try another lap. Did you beat your previous time?

End of race	No overtaking – **ADD 5 seconds.**
Pull aside, faster car overtaking – **ADD 3 seconds.**	You have broken race rules – **you are OUT** of the race.
Oil or water on the track – **ADD 10 seconds**	A hazard has been removed – **SUBTRACT 1 second.**

Your car has a problem – **make a pit stop ADD 4 seconds.**

CHALLENGE QUESTIONS

You are travelling at 201 km (125 mph) when there is an accident up ahead.

Drivers cannot stop straight away. To stop safely, they need time to think and then time to brake. Look at the STOPPING DISTANCES chart.

a) If a car is about 4 metres long, how many car lengths does it take to stop if you are travelling at 64 km (40 mph)?

b) What about if you are travelling at 113 km (70 mph)?

c) The *thinking distances* are in a multiplication table. Which one?

STOPPING DISTANCES

Speed (km)		Thinking distance (metres)	Braking distance (metres)	Total stopping distance (metres)
32 km	(20 mph)	6	6	12
48 km	(30 mph)	9	14	23
64 km	(40 mph)	12	24	36
80 km	(50 mph)	15	38	53
97 km	(60 mph)	18	55	73
113 km	(70 mph)	21	75	96

TUNNEL

MAKE A NINE SECOND PIT STOP

Your car's fuel tank is nearly empty and your tyres need changing. It is time to make a **pit stop.** Your pit crew will only take an incredible 9 seconds to refuel the car, change four wheels and check for any damage. But you will add a mighty 29 seconds to your lap time because you will have to slow down to drive in and out of the **pits** – so the faster you can make your pit stop the better! **Formula One** refuelling equipment supplies fuel so fast, it could fill the tank of a normal family car in about 4 seconds! You are now in the pits, sit back and let your expert crew do what they do best.

DRIVER ASSESSMENT

There are 18 people in your pit crew:
- *3 people per wheel to remove the old wheel and fit the new wheel.*
- *2 people to operate the front and rear **jacks**.*
- *2 people to operate the refuelling rig and base.*
- *1 person to display the lollipop.*
- *1 person to clean your visor.*

1) How many crew members work on the wheels?
2) In twenty teams of 18 people how many are wheel changers?
3) In twenty teams of 18 people how many help put in the fuel?

Refuelling needs to happen fast. It takes 1 second to put 12 litres of fuel into a Formula One car's fuel tank. You need to put in about 108 litres of fuel at your pit stop.

4) Can this be done in 9 seconds?

Into the pits to make a pit stop.

CHALLENGE QUESTIONS

READY, STEADY, GO!
See how fast you can work by doing these quickfire challenges. Perhaps ask a friend to time you.
YOU ONLY HAVE 5 SECONDS FOR EACH:

a) Recite the x4 table.
b) Sum the first four even numbers starting with 2.
c) Say how many centimetres there are in a kilometre.
d) Sum 19, 20 and 21.

(Try these challenges, then look at page 29. You will find TIPS to help you sum and recite times tables.)

RACE FACT

The only speed limit at a **Grand Prix** is in the pit lane. During a practice session, a driver can be fined £150 for each km/h over the speed limit he goes! The cars have speed limiters which the driver activates as soon as he drives into the pit lane. He does this by pressing a button on the steering wheel.

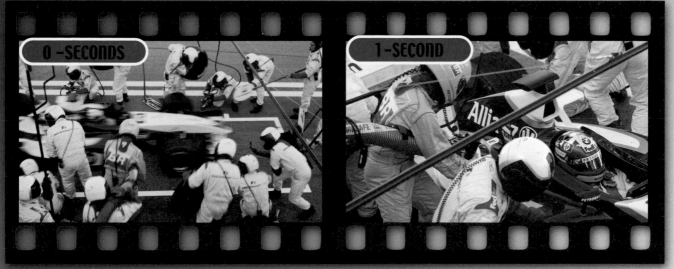

0 –SECONDS

Car hits marks in pit lane. The driver is held in place by a lollipop man.

1–SECOND

The crew start undoing the wheel nuts, while the front and rear jack men raise the car off the jacks. The refueller connects with the car. A crew member cleans the driver's visor.

2–SECONDS

Wheel crew remove old tyres, while other wheel crew members get the new tyres in place.

3/4 SECONDS

Wheel gun members tighten up the wheel nuts. As each wheel crew finish their job they raise their hand to indicate they have finished.

5–SECONDS

The car is dropped from its jacks. The lollipop man tells the driver to select first gear and get ready to go.

7/8/9–SECONDS

The refuelling is finished and the crew remove the fuel hose. The lollipop man lifts his signal up and the driver shoots off.

Congratulations – you won the **Monaco Grand Prix.** You earned yourself 10 points, the maximum number of points available, and you stood on the winner's podium spraying champagne over your cheering fans. Since Monaco, you have been in the top eight in every race. It is now nearing the end of the season and there are just three Grands Prix left. *The Drivers' World Championship* will be won by the driver with the most points at the end of the season. Take your final DRIVER ASSESSMENT and work out what you will need to do to become World Champion.

DRIVER ASSESSMENT

On page 27 you will see three DATA BOXES.

• The points a driver can earn in a race.
• The points earned by the drivers so far this season.
• The points for the final three Grands Prix of the season.

Look at the information carefully, then try answering these questions:

1) In what position did the BMW Williams F1 driver finish in the Chinese Grand Prix?
2) In what position did you finish in the Japanese Grand Prix?
3) After all the races, the Renault driver finished with a total of 51 points. In what position was he in the Japanese Grand Prix?
4) Does BAR or McLaren finish with more points at the end of the season? How many more?
5) What position must you finish in the Brazilian Grand Prix in order to win the World Championship?

CHAMPION FACT

Michael Schumacher is the most successful world champion in history. At the end of the 2003 season, he had won a record six Drivers' World Championships – 1994, 1995, 2000, 2001, 2002 and 2003.

CHAMPION FACT

Renault's Fernando Alonso has proved he is a champion of the future. At the 2003 Hungary Grand Prix, he became the youngest ever race winner.

POINTS

Points are awarded to the drivers as follows:

Position in race

Position	Points
1st	10 points
2nd	8 points
3rd	6 points
4th	5 points
5th	4 points
6th	3 points
7th	2 points
8th	1 point

POINTS SO FAR THIS SEASON

DRIVER	POINTS SO FAR
BMW WilliamsF1 Driver	73
YOU	70
BAR Driver	55
McLaren Driver	47
Ferrari Driver	68
Renault Driver	41

POINTS FOR THE FINAL THREE GRANDS PRIX OF THE SEASON

DRIVER	CHINA GP	JAPAN GP	BRAZIL GP
BMW WilliamsF1 Driver	4	10	6
YOU	8	6	??
BAR Driver	1	4	0
McLaren Driver	3	5	0
Ferrari Driver	10	8	4
Renault Driver	6	??	1

The chequered flag signals the end of the race.

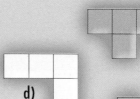

It's champagne time for the winners!

CHALLENGE QUESTION

At the edge of the track, workers are building the winner's podium! The people building the podium have brought flat packs that they can fold to make boxes to stand on.

Which of these are **nets** which would make up into an open topped box?

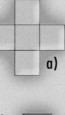

a) b) c) d) e) f)

(You will find some more information about SHAPES on page 29)

TIPS FOR MATHS SUCCESS

PAGES 6–7

DRIVER ASSESSMENT

TIP: *"Find the difference between"* is another way of saying subtract. We need to subtract (or take away) the smaller number from the larger number to find the difference.

PAGES 8–9

DRIVER ASSESSMENT

Using data in a pictogram:

A **pictogram** is a chart where a picture is used to show several units. In the pictogram on page 8, a picture of a complete wheel stands for five laps of the circuit.

Pictures can be cut into **fractions**, so this picture shows two laps.

CHALLENGE QUESTIONS
Rounding whole numbers and decimal fractions:

When rounding numbers and **decimal fractions** we always follow the same rules:
36 rounded to the nearest ten is 40 because we round up numbers that end in 5, 6, 7, 8 or 9.
We round down numbers that end in 4, 3, 2 or 1.
For example, 32 would be rounded down to 30.

When rounding decimal fractions to the nearest whole number, we use the same rules:
so 3.6 is rounded to 4 and 3.2 is rounded to 3.

(The lap lengths in the Grand Prix circuits DATA BOX have all been rounded to the nearest tenth.)

PAGES 10–11

DRIVER ASSESSMENT

TIP: There are 60 seconds in a minute.

CHALLENGE QUESTIONS

TIP: There are 60 minutes in one hour.

PAGES 12–13

CHALLENGE QUESTIONS

Understanding division:
TIP: Dividing by 100 is the same as dividing by 10 and by 10 again.

PAGES 14–15

CHALLENGE QUESTION

Making turns and measuring angles:
Angles are a measure of turn. Angles are measured in **degrees**. The symbol for degrees is °.

One whole turn (a complete revolution) is 360°.

A quarter turn is 90° or one *right angle*.

There are four *right angles* in one whole turn.

The angles at the corners of squares and rectangles always measure 90°.

PAGES 16–17

CHALLENGE QUESTIONS

Measuring perimeter:

TIP: With rectangles you can work out the **perimeter** in three different ways:

- Add all four sides.
- Add one long and one short side and then double the answer.
- Double the length of the long side then double the length of the short side and add the totals together.

The perimeter of this rectangle is 16 m.

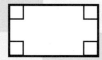

5 m

3 m   3 m

5 m

PAGES 18–19

CHALLENGE QUESTION

Ordering numbers:

When we put things in order 1st (first), 2nd (second), 3rd (third), 4th (fourth) and so on, we are using *ordinal numbers*.
Counting numbers 1, 2, 3, 4 and so on, are called *cardinal numbers*.

PAGES 20–21

Looking for patterns:

The pattern of lights on page 21 is interesting. Patterns are important in maths.
Always look for patterns in numbers and shapes. For example, in the 5 x table, the answers always end in 5 or 0.

Find out about the pattern in normal traffic lights that you see on the road. What comes after red?

PAGES 24–25

CHALLENGE QUESTIONS

x4 TABLE:

TIP: Reciting the x4 table could be done using just the products: 4, 8, 12, 16, 20 and so on.

Summing:

Summing numbers is often easier when the order is changed.
In the challenges we are adding 2, 4, 6, and 8. 8 and 2 make 10, and so do 4 and 6.

Summing 19, 20 and 21 can be done quickly by realising that it is the same as 3 x 20 because taking the 1 from 21 and adding it to the 19 makes three 20s!

PAGES 26–27

CHALLENGE QUESTION

Investigating shapes:

Squares fitted together so that they touch along at least one side are called *polyominoes*.
Polyominoes made of five squares, are named *pentominoes*. Here are 12 pentominoes, eight of them will fold up into a box with an open top.

UNITS OF MEASUREMENT

We use two systems of measurement in the UK: *metric* (centimetres, metres, kilometres, grams, kilograms) and *imperial* (inches, feet, miles, ounces, pounds).

METRIC		IMPERIAL	
Length		**Length**	
1 millimetre (mm)		1 inch (in)	
1 centimetre (cm)	= 10 mm	1 foot (ft)	= 12 in
1 metre (m)	= 100 cm	1 yard (yd)	= 3 ft
1 kilometre (km)	= 1000 m	1 mile	= 1760 yd
Weight		**Weight**	
1 gram (g)		1 ounce (oz)	
1 kilogram (kg)	= 1000 g	1 pound (lb)	= 16 oz
1 tonne (t)	= 1000 kg	1 ton	= 2240 lb
Capacity		**Capacity**	
1 millilitre (ml)		1 fluid ounce (fl oz)	
1 centilitre (cl) = 10 ml		1 UK pint (pt)	= 20 fl oz
1 litre (l) = 1000 ml		1 UK gallon (gal)	= 8 pt

Comparing metric and imperial measurements:

1 kilometre = 0.62 of a mile
1 kilogram = 2.2 pounds
0.57 litre = 1 UK pint

PAGES 6–7

DRIVER ASSESSMENT

1) The shortest distance is 320 km (199 miles) to Monza in Italy.
   The longest distance is 16 404 km (10 193 miles) to Melbourne in Australia.
2) 4841 km (3008 miles)   3) 5823 km (3618 miles)
4) 573 km (356 miles)   5) 4110 km (2554 miles)

CHALLENGE QUESTIONS

a) The month on the driver's calendar is July.
b) The driver is racing in Great Britain at the Silverstone circuit on the second Sunday (11 July).

PAGES 8–9

DRIVER ASSESSMENT

The number of laps shown in the **pictogram** for each of the Grands Prix is:

Australia	58 laps	USA	73 laps
Malaysia	56 laps	Gt Britain	60 laps
San Marino	62 laps	Italy	53 laps
Europe	60 laps		

CHALLENGE QUESTIONS

a) Europe and Great Britain
b) Malaysia, Italy, China and Japan

PAGES 10–11

DRIVER ASSESSMENT

1) Your times have improved in cycling by 15 seconds, and in running, by 21 seconds.
2) Your swimming time has got slower. You will need to improve your time by 6 seconds to match last season.

CHALLENGE QUESTIONS

a) You spent 9 hours 35 minutes each week in the gym.
b) You spent 22 hours training each week.

PAGES 12–13

DRIVER ASSESSMENT

1) The width of the car is about 1800 mm.
2) The length of the car is approximately 370 cm.
3) The weight of the car and driver is at least 605 kg.

CHALLENGE QUESTIONS

a) 24 000 hours work each person.
b) 2400 hours work each person.
c) 800 hours work each person.
d) 80 days

PAGES 14–15

DRIVER ASSESSMENT

1) Your summing should show that a HIGH **downforce** (wing setting) gives the fastest lap time.

DOWNFORCE	LAP TIME (SECONDS)
LOW setting	75.3
MEDIUM setting	74.7
HIGH setting	**74.6**

2) Your summing should show that LOW gear settings give the fastest lap time.

GEAR SETTINGS	LAP TIME (SECONDS)
LOW setting	**74.4**
MEDIUM setting	74.5
HIGH setting	74.8

CHALLENGE QUESTION

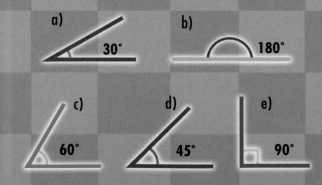

a) 30°   b) 180°
c) 60°   d) 45°   e) 90°

PAGES 16—17

DRIVER ASSESSMENT

1) You will need 117 kg of fuel at the start of the race.
2) You will put in 78 kg of fuel at your first pit stop.
3) You will need to put in 57 kg of fuel at the first and second pit stops and 63 kg of fuel at the third pit stop.

CHALLENGE QUESTIONS

a) The **perimeter** fence would be 6 km 890 m.
b) The perimeter of the rectangle is 15 cm.
c) The length of each side of the **regular hexagon** is 5 cm.

PAGES 18—19

DRIVER ASSESSMENT

1) *CAR 3* sets off 3 minutes after 2:00 pm.
2) *CAR 11* sets off 19 minutes after 2:00 pm.
3) *CAR 16* sets off 28½ minutes after 2:00 pm.
4) *YOUR CAR* sets off 34½ minutes after 2:00 pm.

CHALLENGE QUESTION

6th **BAR driver** (75.4 seconds)

5th **Ferrari driver** (75.1 seconds)

4th **McLaren driver** (75.0 seconds)

3rd **Renault driver** (74.9 seconds)

2nd **YOU** (74.8 seconds)

POLE **BMW WilliamsF1 driver** (74.6 seconds)

PAGES 20—21

DRIVER ASSESSMENT

The driver's morning should be in this order:
Photo B: Eat breakfast 8:30 am
Photo E: Meeting with engineers 9:30 am
Photo F: Drivers' parade 11:30 am
Photo A: Meet reporters 12:00 pm
Photo D: Put on helmet 1:20 pm
Photo C: Make final checks on car 1:50 pm

CHALLENGE QUESTION

The team have exactly 3 hours 6 minutes of repairs to make. Your car will be ready in time!

PAGES 22—23

CHALLENGE QUESTIONS

a) 9 car lengths   b) 24 car lengths
c) x 3 table (3, **6**, **9**, **12**, **15**, **18**, **21**, 24, 27, 30, 33, 36)

PAGES 24—25

DRIVER ASSESSMENT

1) 12 crew members work on the wheels.
2) 240 people are wheel changers.
3) 40 people put in the fuel.
4) Yes — it takes exactly 9 seconds to fill up with 108 litres of fuel.

PAGES 26—27

DRIVER ASSESSMENT

1) The BMW WilliamsF1 driver finished 5th (fifth).
2) You finished 3rd (third) in the Japanese Grand Prix.
3) The Renault driver finished 6th (sixth).
4) BAR finishes with 5 more points.
5) YOU must finish 1st (first) to win the World Championship

CHALLENGE QUESTION

The blue **nets** can be made up into an open topped box (a, b, e and f).

a) c) e)
b) d) f)

GLOSSARY

CHASSIS The main bodies of the cars.

CONSTRUCTORS The team who build and race a Formula One car. Formula One rules state that constructors are a team or individuals who must design and build the car.

DOWNFORCE An effect caused by the 'wings' on a Formula One car. The wings are on the nose and back of the car. They are set up to force the car to stick to the road. This is the opposite effect to an aircraft's wings that are set up to lift the aircraft off the ground.

FORMULA ONE A set of rules for single seater racing cars. The rules specify the design of the cars and the safety measures they must have.

GRAND PRIX A long distance car or motorbike race. One of a series held in different countries.

GRID The start of a Formula One race. The cars line up in pairs in staggered rows. There is 8 metres between each row.

JACKS Portable pieces of equipment that are used to raise a car off the ground so that its wheels can be changed.

PIT STOPS Visits to the pits during a race. The car can be checked, refuelled and fitted with new wheels. Cars also make pit stops if they have a mechanical problem during a race.

PITS An area just off the race track where the racing teams' mechanics can work on the cars, before and during a race.

PRESS CONFERENCES Group meetings where journalists and radio and TV broadcasters are able to interview the racing teams and drivers.

QUALIFYING SESSION A timed session of laps. The times of these laps are used to work out the position of each car on the grid.

SPONSOR A company which pays a Formula One team to have their name displayed in high visibility places on the teams' cars and the drivers' clothing. This makes money for the Formula One team enabling them to spend huge amounts of money on their cars.

STRATEGY A plan of action.

MATHS GLOSSARY

2-D (TWO DIMENSIONAL) Flat with length (or height) and width, but no depth (thickness)

3-D (THREE DIMENSIONAL) Shapes that have length (or height), width and depth (thickness).

ANGLES Measures of turn.

DECIMAL FRACTIONS We use a counting system involving tens, multiples of ten and fractions of ten. The decimal point separates whole numbers from decimal fractions. *For example, in the number 672.53, 5 is tenths and 3 is hundredths.*

DEGREES The units used for measuring angles and temperatures.

ESTIMATE To find a number or amount that is close to an exact answer.

FRACTIONS These are made when shapes or numbers are cut into equal parts. For example, if a shape is cut into four equal parts, each part is one whole divided by four, or a quarter (¼).

HEXAGON A 2-D (two-dimensional) shape with six straight sides and six angles.

NET A 2-D (flat) shape that can be folded to make a 3-D shape.

PERIMETER The distance all the way around a shape.

PICTOGRAM In a pictogram pictures are used to show information.

REGULAR Used to describe 2-D shapes which have sides that are equal in length and 3-D shapes with faces all the same in shape and size.

t=top, b=bottom, c=centre, l=left, r=right, OFC=outside front cover, OBC=outside back cover

Alamy: 20bc. Redzone Motorsport Images (John Marsh): 1, 11c, 12-13, 15, 18-19, 20tr, 21cl, 21bl, 26-27main, OBC.
Sporting Pictures: 9, 11t, 11b, 16-17, 20br, 20bl, 23, 24-25, 27cr.

Every effort has been made to trace the copyright holders, and we apologize in advance for any unintentional omissions.
We would be pleased to insert the appropriate acknowledgements in any subsequent edition of this publication.